How Yesterday's Dream Held Her

LA BREA M. SPIVEY

Cover Illustration by Angela M. Maxson

All the material in this book has appeared for the first time in 2018 with the exception of:
Anna's Leap 1ST printing 2017 in the
Artifact Nouveau. Spring 2017 Volume 3 Issue 2
A Writer's Guild Publication
Fragile Strength, 24th Annual Dance Poetry Festival 2017

Library Of Congress Control Number: 2018902887

Printed in the United States of America

ISBN-13:978-0-692-07343-8

DEDICATION

To my former professor Paula Sheil, who inspired me to continue writing poems.

To my children Kellyce and Khiyuri, thank you for your continuous patience in this process.

TABLE OF CONTENTS

NEST IT

An alchemy stone in a
Bluebirds nest; a binary home that may
Cost you
Death. The order reversed, spiraling out of control
Empty and
Forever my lady, fuck me gracefully.
God as you've heard of, Gaia you do not know, yet
Hiding from justice she is king.
Iron dreams dimensional magic
Justified by its deception.
Kemet fucked, a bowel stain still stands its portality
Liven up songs inside the dome
Mathematically though.
Nearly all of us, like worms, crawl through dirt
Ordained by threat.
Put an owl on a branch is does not trust
Quantumly figure how much.
"Roger that", said the
Serpent of cure,
"Tomorrow an aerie will be no more".
Ultrapure the sparrow fly's to meet the

Venerable
Wren, they share a flame.
X marks the spark
Y chromosome taps the
Zen of a philosopher's stone in a bluebirds nest.

FOUGHT OF MY HONE

Sitting on my sofa in my old home
Brightly lit by sun rays, no sign fire had burned it.
I searched for the address, home
Shuffling through papers, seeing names, numbers,
    geometric shapes
Frustrated, realizing the least of the matter
Found nothing useful, emotions led out of confine
Night reflected my mood inward, most darkest
Stars discerned my essence, provided a map, and called me
    up.
Reaching for the glitter above my head before my eyes
Swept by fate, straight alike a pole, rocketed, rammed into
    darkness
Familiar kaleidoscope focus, darkness forms its colors
    shiny.
Still forging upward my face tore through waters
Curled upside down, deep into Adam's ale, my back then
    fell, crashing against it
Of momma and Gaia I flipped to soar where my map had
    formed a boundless panorama descry.
Its tears drew me through the midst its beauty.

There I'd join the nakedness of all my mothers, our heart,
our voice.
No air was evident, however, I had breathed.
A bridges wooden planks and thick rope met my bare feet,
would guide me over to the lea I knew all too well.
Life handed me a spear; a torch around her neck,
magnetic, instrumented me ahead.
Looking back I noticed my slumber, a darkness without
sand
A course given with my lance and happy feet caught up to
muddy waters.
Her tone carried my youthfulness, sounded like caresses.

"Use your spear, there is something there."

Eyes saw the face of a princess beneath the swamp, my
gaff had purpose.
Into the mud and out at the end, a crocodile. The unclean
pastures led a way out, into a love grounded for
play
Magnetic copper tones filled the amusement.
Gently, I touched the hand of us, her grasp awarded
mines.
Oceans expressed grand abundance, laughter sang its own
songs

HOW YESTERDAY'S DREAM HELD HER

A unicellular feast of life; anew the experience born again I
had been.
Though surrender had a crisis to avert
Clouded by the dust from a hammered coffin nail, wind
brought with it what appeared to resemble a small
city park.
The difference, a turbulent witnessed my own limitations.
That bridge must be crossed again, having faced the
dragon, and again, next time with trident.

INJURY

I slept once worried
Faded feeling so
Sorry outdated depressed

In goose down and through
Slips of injury
Woke now too deliberate

Gaveling, once!, twice!
Hypocritical
Unrobed of every hurt

ANNA'S LEAP

It looked like sugar from far away,
Godard's hawks on linen curtains in Mumbai.
Anna's jet black bob brushed her shoulders as she turned
    to hear how yesterday's dream held her;
Release the black bear to catch the red fish
Die and swim in the Atlantic
Drown that suspicious notion and meet Nuti Curmudgeon
Tell this all it needs to know, then awake from above your
    pillow
Selfless chant pumping heart
Anna lead like navigational art
Come here white wolf, go there wild hog
Anna take a leap like a South American bullfrog

SINCERELY…

Hey,

I haven't been pleasant. I apologize for being distant. I've suffered many losses, left to figure out why it was necessary to have experienced them. Lots of work had to be done, had to do it alone. An abundance of life has led me ever since. Things were sweet, great! But the thought of never reconciling with you moved me. I wouldn't dare go any further without your loyal hand. You protected me, then, now and forever. Our fates must be joined. You matter just as our distance at once. I appreciate you. More now than ever I miss you, I need you, because I love you. At least for now, may we keep in touch? Later, meet in the middle? Forever, bow tie our relationship, seal our destiny?

Sincerely,

Her

ANNA'S YESTERDAY

Anna, quiet destroyer of the warmth
Creeping through evenings after noon
A calm renewal of wellness, serenest vice
When the wind dies west

She remembers the dance sincerely
In laughter, in growth
Liberating decompressions reward
At south shores bay

Her sounds of freshness frees joy to sing
What a heart might find;
Promises in exchange for patience
While relax farewells its presence

HIGH NOON

Twice the time taken to trouble the threat
Tiered, the treetop in bloom
Obstruction offers some obedient
One organ out of oppression real soon

Of the clouds dreams decay
Democracy deals delay
Death delivers deliverance
Known an empathetic age

Attention world!
Too, apathetic sleepers mind
Reflection on yesterday's yeses
Today robbed of its redemption

Trice the time taken to trouble threat
Tiered, the treetop when in bloom

BLACKWELL

Black sage

Pass the jazz fever

Immunize her so she sustains

Through hell and high waters

Black Sabbath

Actualize the unconventional

Cry for coupled rope, so that they

May tap dance on the way

Black tantrum

Boil the soup

Pour in her the nourishment

And fill her with grace

Black velvet

Call all knights

Lead them to our fields

To fecundate their essence

Blackwell

Use her to spring dry wells

And quench the thirst

Of our wandering people

I AM THAT

Nobody whispers, “I am that.”
That in which whistles a fine tune or fright
Every aspect of a mortal combat
An instrument one snaps his fingers with
Or your friendly opponent you must fight
Nobody whispers, “I am that.”
How scrolls unroll when the rubber loops snap
The dust that is kicked up in the sunlight
Every aspect of a mortal combat
That constant rendering of tit for tat
Journeys that rewrite the way of foresight
Nobody whispers, “I am that.”
Distraction from flies or buffalo gnats
Why you grunt when clearing your eyesight
Every aspect of a mortal combat
Always, infinite, I am that
A reward, a loss, the challenge of life
Nobody whispers, “I am that”,
Every aspect of a mortal combat

IGNORE RANT

Silent treatment, fine, say nothing
Only I hear you very well
Your eyes roll of disgust
Your nostrils flare of discomfort
Your head is down for why?
Have you held secrets?
Fix your frown
You show up ugly
Walk away, fine, kick rocks
Seeing your back I assume you're afraid
Your fists balled show resistance
You hold back tears, so that I won't see them?
You cry inside, and store your anger
You're prideful
You deny vulnerability
Only vulnerable is exactly how you are
An easy read becomes prey eventually
A wolf too for we know where he'll go
Slam the door, fine, put yourself away
I can still hear you breathing
Yours pound with leers distasteful stare
Or is it that little child steering, begging, she is key?
Silent treatment, sure stay quiet

Only I know you're hot as hell
Yes, brume the mirror completely
Hopefully when you calm and the mirror clears, for the first time
You'll realize why I am here.

COME AS YOU ARE

At a time all it took was to stand up, show up, be
It hasn't been easy of course, hit after hit
"Life ain't fair", say you
Life was never meant to be fair, rather simply
Endurance is a son of a bitch, and you're still here
Walk as if you yourself crafted Heaven and Earth
Nothing wrong with that
Creatin' as you comin' and goin'
So long (as you come as you are)
Hold on, stay up, burst through the remnants
Of the trials that trail fare
As dainty as you might feel at times
Life will always persist, don't resist
Contour your quarters from within, create space unbound
IT IS YOURS
Initiate forgiveness, yourself, let it be (enough)
Become a motion sense
Have mercy on those misleading hits, bruise their heels
I DARE YOU
Give yourself authority, come as you are
ALL-ready-self-approved

TASTE OF ANSWER

It tastes like turquoise
Perfumed tang, copper, and charcoal
Poison sweetly swallowed
It's awfully ugly, a portrait perfectly painted
Brushed with soil and trim
The blues, its New Grass revival
Sun tints over lands' dye
As the hour changes, wounds are colored
With a delicious grace
Then plays accordingly
To travel verses of tolerated beats and back
Again for victory
True when secrets snuff of greedy ends
The kind of non-sense justified in finally grasping gingers
    tasty fruit
The Bodhi that comes with it, beauty that always delivers
Its polarity produces the orange juice
Sweet, sour, and bitter after a while
A quench longed for turns least thirsty
Deliverance of humility, a cup full of tenderness
Without question its taste has been stretched rhythmically
    around the rim

Flavor of song, have been all along, the very course
denied

WANDER

I wander when you journey
I wonder when you'll know me
Here I am simply, in all places
There I am in the midst of movements' stillness, atop the
bottom, in all bodies of elements; the emission in
which you knew, remembering to make the call

Many is in me and me is in many
I am much in all. Much can be seen of me in your essence.
Your journey's tranquil loudly seek me
I am wonder when you journey, wandering still, found.

Simply in time, when there is none for you to be concerned with, I am that you journey, the way of your honest eye, the sharpest tool you carry.

ENVISION YOUR STAR

Among entertainers who might one be?
Suppose you had a star, one you could keep
Insignificant the fame
More important, purpose, and no praise
What might one be?
Say, a dancer falling rhythmically?
A teacher educating their students' screams?
The lazy handle, gripped by attitudes?
Maybe judged for one's fearlessness?
Would you lead rather than sing?
Who might one serve with starlight today?
Between lines what will one shout?
A hand full of persuasion or doubt?
How about your delivery from scene to applauding scene?
Among entertainers who, what, might one be, articulating
the fundamentals, starring, without the need?

AM I I AM

The reflection face upward your mirrah
Orion's belt that whips sand above your serifs
The show performing her own star uniquely spread over
seas
The process in which *will* spirals best
AM I
I AM
Headed the way intromotionally
A beastern drag on, gold falling from underneath my scales
The wild idea that carries the wind, shaping my destiny
Where treasures journey to know me
AM I
I AM
Strength who named courage and endurance
A leader conceived of righteousness, better yet, and still
Child of absolute, blank, St. Truth and *Is* where
Crying to slap my friend and family into favor

AM I

I AM

One of all portrayals impressed by the refractive essence of
the most high, who came, who speaks, and will
always be the sharpest pose in every eye of my
glamour

I AM

AN UGLY HERO

Ugly proposed a union with Her
Her focus on the black and white gingham drapery
Questioned how something so beautiful be hung so ugly
Ugly proposed a union with Her
Wanderlust about the picture behind the curtains, an odd
    scene Her became aware of
A girl, drowning, and slowly disappearing into the vault
Ugly proposed a union with Her
Afraid to lose sight of the girl, to be saved
Her proposed that ugly wait
Questioned of how someone so beautiful be ignored so
    ugly
Ugly proposed a union with Her
Despaired, Her thought to have lost the chance to be hero,
    and accepted ugly's proposal
Ugly kissed Hers lips
A rush of troubled wind consumed Hers heart
An expansion of newness rose within Her
Ugly's persistence reflected in the sky from the window,
    She is beautiful

LEAVE NO DREAM UNHEARD

Most night's rest is shaken by some knowledge unknown. To sleep she knew she fell, alone. In the middle of the hallway she saw, in formation, souls lined, one following another, walking, passed away. Grounded by the weight of mystification she tuned into what they whispered.

"Anew the land, here", she heard.
One wore a red dress, draped, mesmerizing! Sparkles!
Blinding!
The click of high heels resonated a memory. She knew not until then, she remembered. From the hallway she walked to her bedroom when fear flew through her comprehension, although familiar, cradled her reality. The morning rose with a mustard glow, whispers of the north wind, chiming shades a sparkling red gown.

THUNDER CALLS THE DEPTH

Quietly, Saffiya sat at the foot of my bed
I rested calmly, insomnipresent with eyes wide shut
From outside the window the cool of the electricity
        embraced my wake
A blue wolf whimpered playing instruments in the deep
        magnetic dark
Its call tore through Saffiya's turquatesoteric organ
Afflatus blew bouquet moon lit path
"I am with you always, my scent you see, get into it.
Your ignorance I will disrupt if you chose intentions attention, I warn you."
Presence had split, sharply the Blue co-signed,
"I am with Saffiya, she is therefore that I am. Listen to my thunder absorb its kiss, bow with heads of order."
Now at my side Saffiya branded me mindless; a nothing
        and a recognition, a fragment and a witness
Suddenly a wind whipped through the curtains, the sound
        reflected such event
Remarkable, the mirror without words expressed to whom
        I had died
It saw me, and there I am.

HOW YESTERDAY'S DREAM HELD HER

I'd awakened to the crisp breeze of ripe ball fruit and
cascade mist before, but this was a long overdue
introduction to myself

FRAGILE STRENGTH

Bare,
The bosom of her fragility lay sickly insomniprsent within
the pound that bear all, her advantage.
Exposed, her ignominy, the streaks, stripes, and stains of a
scarlet set in her wake.
She'd sentenced herself to an expire made uneasy.
For all the blatant inadequacies, running, pity.
Without trial an injury discerned her capacity to peacefully
rest
Her last words I would descry,
"The truth will set you free."
Full of electricity, that final breath tore through my aura
then known to me.
Every word made me blue.
I felt delicate, lamented, helpless against the threat of a
thorough absorption, as to how being tried with
trauma is a favor
If only I had not witnessed would I have experienced what
she had? So I thought.
Without anyone to console me, I pondered her last breath
I got intuit shun my ignorance now disrupted
I choose to be warned of a thunderless end
I fished for every hurt my aches could stand

HOW YESTERDAY'S DREAM HELD HER

Cried for each fragment on purpose
I shared all my secrets, dressed myself with forgiveness in
front of all my tormentors
I danced holding hands with the streaks, stripes, and stains
Insomnipresent, and as if butter were between my grip, I
let go
I left blatant inadequacies, running, pity unclaimed for
liberties sake
Remarkable, the bosom of my strength within the pound
that bear all; simple, split, yet whole, a memory
and a disregard lay rested, forgiven with honor,
our advantage.
Her streaks, stripes, and stains recognized a thunderous
life; my fragile strength.

WHAT I'D KEEP

Beats that resonate when beauties inner twine
Spirits' fire, burning on the way home
Yes, the expression of such truth
The savoring taste of noise that silence has written
Young land, old mountains, my resting spot above all the resistance
Shallow, deep waters, and the stillness between them
Control in the presence of doubt
You, if you let me

KNOW ANSWER

Before her mother pushed her out from the womb, began
the journey
It will be her experiences in this way that she remembers
how all, she knew
Her mission has always been to question everything
Many answers, more questions, grasping much, knowing
nothing absolutely.
An identity she's chased, hoped along the way to catch
virtue
Individuality, that one-of-a-kind uniqueness, worth, and
significance
Glimpses denied her an introduction
Emotions raged disorder, she gave up her position as
investigator to reform her experiences
One traumatic catastrophe after another paralyzed her
emotions
All cried out, asking if her life were real, her desire to know
disappeared
She thought not of a God or anything, her heart cast her
body to rest
Exhaustion breathed her memory away. Sleep had crept,
but never took its place
A moment made itself aware, and all she knew asked her,

"How?"

GRASP

I am not you
Although I see myself well within you
You can be like me, I highly advise it
But you know not, how you are
Lost, and without recognition
Believing in me, with little to know understanding
My story is his in every aspect of the word
Hers, whole, misspelled, and split in two
His story then, now, and forever history
Your story is yesterday, create a new one, again let it go
Only then, ever being his tree (a giving portion)
Blooming how life writes any story

NAVIGATIONAL ART

Sweet fire of revision, I come to revitalize your destination
I've heard your tales
I've heard your cries and the lies you've discerningly
ignored
The red fish has caught your attention
Your fears have been bathed in the Atlantic journey to
work in your flavor
I've held you for so long
Before your mothers memory would consume you
The Deja Vudoo matters no more, Saffiya's dream still and
always awaits your turn
Thank you for introspection kept
The silence and the grasp of your first cry, forever
nourishing the core that holds you
The call has been made; a kiss has set sail
Let us move before the seed is hallowed, and our inner
wheel swallowed

CATASTROPHE THE GREAT

Her impatience provoked the sun's greater later
Rise, beam, and fall
Burning strength into a beauty
Branding moral tattoo

Her curiosity made a child of the moon
Freedom waited for her truth, and with greater faith
A far up seed, twinkling spirit, free
Having her way at laughter

Such wonder a child made greater later
Wore out an ideas hole to penetrate
Choice at the darkest of moments
Where shadows appeared to wait, for a chance, eclipsed,
then great

DREAM

The ironing board trembled. Neighbors' footsteps clomped quickly beyond the streets, people screamed, dogs whined, gates rattled.

The iron printed a stain on her silk green blouse. From the window water had come through. Both her babies she grabbed, strapping them each in her arms.

Mothers, fathers, children and pets ran through the city. They ran!

She ran!

Raging water destroying everything in its path. A flood had come to wipe them out. Behind and above her waves high. Hitting corners and alley's, lots and fences, she ran with her babies. She was soon met by fire from the neighboring city, burning all in its way to ash. With waves rushing and heat ablaze closing in on her family, her ears rang, their screams faded.

To her left a vacant bank, her right a field of familiar black sheep, welcoming their time of death. The ground warm below her.

A paralyzing fear and surrender struck at once. In a sweat and chills all through her body, gasping for air, she'd awaken at home to see how her tears, frustration, and exhaustion had forced them to sleep, her babies next to her, right up under her arms.

A MATCH FOR THE MIX

Of the last hand full of nights something quite surprising
A sign had brought her the swift psalm across high cheek bone
A boost, a call, the sermon of grasping; a way worth more than going.
A journey in which possessed its own whips, dungeons, and tethers at the turning point had caught her
Her face directed at redemption, salvation, and desire; an illusory match lit for the mix
Such a hit forced her to groan in her weary
Time and time again the trip was threatening, deadly even
While waiting for the swift psalm, the rhythm of her foolishness approached
With rage and eyes to see she struck back
Calling out ways she's traveled before
Branded by fire she burst into tears, burnt, hurt, and paved with yet another way

LOVE BELOW

Upon this boat
I ride a love below
My hands writing the tides
Paddles erase the waves
Eyes know something about the deep
My hands want to see
How shallow the light appears
How deep the dark can hear
Listening for current turmoil, I receive a love letter
Upon this boat
I ride a love below
My hands knowing the coldest deep

WE KNOW THIS SONG

Startling fortissimo thunder
Lightening loads of wounds
Unwrapping fragments
Souls out of the cold
Singers ringer ringing
That track around the rim
Singing!
Turn up the volume

MOTIF GENE US

Creativity gives time a motif.
Between it and death, death had brushed my hair, tapping
into a fascination that only wonder could
dimension.
Forced into a world of puzzle in pieces, a slice of Momma
kept me.
Her portion created a bowl that I'd soon be flushed, at her
suggestion I chose
The way of orgasmic eruption, her amniotic embrace
housed me.
I'd experienced watching a tiny blue seed expand until I
became it.
This panoramic collection shifted, holding several keys to
my existence.
Unicorns spread like jelly through my veins, developing to
and fro, front and center.
A guide I'd known be foresight, pulsated within.
At once, gemmed and dreamt, fascination electrocuted
senses, magnetizing a point of rejection and return
at what seemed to be ahead.

Time was nothing like losing, and clearance had made its
    way.
I was shot from range when I'd be robbed of my
    knowledge, forgetting the brush with death.
The mysteries know, themselves, that time has a killer,
In a world of puzzle play, some wonder, and creativity can
    bore me breathtaking again.

SEASONED

Four seasons at once
Neptune and moon dare meet the sun
Triggers spread worry
My veins claim change is turning
Dare she, in the midst of a crisis
A wonder love can only be experienced
A gift in the darkest of forecast

TIDES A TRIP

Her life is a song, a song of no words to sing, only waves to dance
She rides alone, a love below, in the middle of the ocean inside a boat
Moving to the chorus of her lessons; an instrumental
Where the tides know too, eagle soar her confidence, fish follow her balance
Wind blows fear away. Dolphins crescent her bow, and a songs performance, never ending
The chorus ever changing, arabesque, she sails, and reaps what breath is left to sow

BABY MAGIC

I can see much and all its expressions
I've traveled far. I've traveled long, not knowing whether or not there really is an end
With no knowledge or the hope of ever becoming, I take the backseat watching mommas tresses
Babysitter of magic, journey's way, my imagination and no sources to confront
Here to witness the intention of my own expressive creativity
By the looks of it, mommas tresses hold my attention, for now an absolute observation. Hair dancing to the winds song, definitely an inspiration

SLITHER

Hidden in the shadows more than just a beast
Awaits an action needing to be taken
Vulnerable and thought to have been in control
It shows up badass bad bad
A friend one dare ignore, Oh what a snake
Big, bad, charming, and clever. Sexy, sneaky, a thief, a liar
But that big badass has served you before, up against the
cruel, ugly, sociopathic, predatory world
Horror hidden in the shadows, more than just that beast
The gates may be forced open
Having you then retreat
Call all fear, and by its many names
Play with these beasts, big badasses, friends
Let them out to stretch, let them shed their skin
It shows up badass bad bad
Be careful mines listens to me
It shows up badass bad bad, oh what a friend

TIIMES WAKING

In waking life

A times a stamp

Morning springs at the split second dial

Night curled under blankets

Eyes wide up and head topped off

Another world unwraps its resting

Here, a times a past patient impression

HUMBLE SWEETER

Made in a world
Just like free
Dreamy and humble
Wings like flamingo
Candy sweet
Sugar
Running through wildly
Humble
Humble world, humble
Just like free
When a nights' dream
Come true, the X set stream

MY DEAR PORTMAN

I can't act like you
Because I adore you
Where the heart is
Reminds me of why
Wild hearts can't be broken
True everyone says I love you
Closer to the garden state
It's anywhere but here
St. Elsewhere is how
We can ace the Ventura
In sweet November
A tale of love and darkness
Reaches the cold mountain
When you will be my ain true love
Kings around the knight of cups
The hymn of the pearl
Whispers the origin of
My blueberry knights
Rings intertwine
Skipping stone plays at the peak
Song to song
The beat of my heart is

Weathered under ground

Mane in the wind

Tail matching mine

I race to meet annihilation

Face to face

Illusions and mirrors

Knocking me off my seat

The death and the life of me

Met by yours truly,

Jackie

SULKED

Yes, it rained
Out in polka dot rain boots
Celebrating every raindrop reunion
Droplets crowds her plum cheeks
Granted, the pond on her tongue
A clumsy twirl and slob too
Amazed at the drip
At a leaves edge
Splash!, its grace anointed her forehead
Giggles made the day fun
Drinking joy from the sky, its clouds
I watched her play
And the rain blended my cry

GRANDMA WHITES HOUSE

A walk on Washington street meant more to me than anything else. Great mommas along that street, around every corner knew all too well, Grandma Whites house was care at its best. Each step welcomed my approach. From the outside, the curtains advertised a new experience; a grand opening to a new surprise. Upon entry, a rush of freshly baked biscuits permeated through and out into the neighborhood.

Greetings given by a stuffed crocodile great grandpa caught himself. The lavish sitting room, a child could only glance.

The grand mirror on the wall framed the reflected tapestry, which complimented piano upright. Great momma said she used to play in her day, and for us little ones to keep our fingers from touching it.

Upholstery wasn't to be sat on by any child that played outside. Blues, flowers, and greenery themed the room. Not a scratch on the cherry, dust didn't exist there. Lamps, crystal bowls, each with candy in it, tempting my little hands.

During the day the sun made its way through, diamondizing the glitter of the interior. Great momma had the most delicate and exquisite taste. More crystal bowls held seashell carved soaps, décor'd the bathroom counter. Shower curtains draped the tub, hiding a small window that was always left cracked allowing the freshness of day, and the crisp of night to charm her Victorian illustrations.

Peaches rang in her bedroom. Peaches and coral pinks bloomed a girls dream come true. Bedspread trimmed with ruffles, shammed pillows resting in place. All made up the dressing table sat close to the window, littered gracefully with a woman's precious accessories, and a brush so soft only a baby could use it.

In another bedroom, the biggest bed I'd ever seen. Big and wide. A thick navy bedspread covered it totally, tailored with tucked pillows, a night stand on either side topped with beautiful shades of sterling. Porcelain dolls filled the mass, their eyes wide open, scary. Great momma would laugh when we hurried down the hallway after her, when passing that room.

Toward the kitchen our little eyes could only view the tall china cupboard and dining table full of mommas finest dishes collected. From there the sight of the kitchen table *I* could sit at made me weak, for there was where I ate mommas freshly baked biscuits. The smell vaporized who I thought I was. I thought every appliance had to be used to create that warm buttery leavened bread.

Homemade strawberry jam, and butter centered the table. I'd sit down as soon as momma grabbed her oven mitten. I'd look into her blue cataract eyes through the cloud of steam rising from them butter ball biscuits. Momma would take a long butter knife and split the biscuit elegantly, catch the moisture with a slice of salted butter, spread it on both pieces for me. The way she spread that jam with a spoon, she'd written a thank you note to the heavenly. A kiss followed as she handed me her mastery. I'd initiate the first bite with a sniff so close my hearing could taste the delicacy. The love cuisine paralyzed every part of my body but my mouth. My head would rest on one hand while the other fed me.

Great mommas biscuits were the breast of momma, mother, her wholesome arms cradling me as I feast on such nourishment. When I was finished, my life was fresh, tired…nappy. Momma knew what she'd been doing. No child of hers could or would ever resist her biscuits.

A nap meant I'd be well rested, and well to contain myself in her garden. The back of the house was where us children could play. Those half brick half wood walls were intimidating, as to be still or careful while running around. The carpet mixed colored shag of ugly, the fireplace a black hole we refused to go near, and the television showing PBS Specials only. I can still see the butterfly flying high.

Off to the side, the slide door opened to the most heavenly garden in the world. The sweetest air transfused my little soul. Oranges, lemons, apples, cherries, and my favorite runners against the fence, strawberries. The grass its greenest, praying mantis standing to lift us afloat. Sun shining its brightest, kissing all. A paradise! Momma would show me how and when to pick the fruit. My two year old Easter basket carried the ones I'd picked.

Everything about great mommas house was harmonious. Every room tranquility. And them biscuits…GOD!!, of the foods.

Being at great mommas house was life. Leaving was having fell upon death with no hope of an afterlife. A walk on Washington street meant we were going to grandma Whites house.

HLBD

It is black, blackest ever!
Jet pitched home run black
Long, she brushes the heels of my soles
An embrace of a lifetime these threads
Thick and contoured, sticky
Voluptuous accents
A line, scooped neck
Coke bottle bumps
Our glass bracelet
Sharp faceted gems
Three quarter sleeves allow for its show
Against a smooth red brown tone
Tune these tricks for green treats in black
This bitch is worth every bit
DAMN!
I look good in
Her little black dress

COME HOME

Broken glass pieced together
The table your mess, its perfection
Mirrors stainless, grand

Lime green sofa shampooed
Two old women wait
Since dawn was due

Children have come to stay
Affection, significance, adventure
All brought toys to share and play

Master rooms of motif, themed and clean
Blues, eclectic gems and unicorns
Wildest dream catchers above a bed for a king

Wardrobe, black
Come home sweetie please

Food in the fridge. Strawberry cheesecake

Moon pies, cookies, Chai tea
Crab, mixed berry punch

There's a journal here with your name on it, it has no entry

HOME

From home to mother's home. Displaced, dependent,
unemployed, worthless
Emotions can't wait. Love to loss of everything worked
for.
Safely comfortable, disrupted, delusional, from calm to
paranoid
Barbeque and burning fire places shake what sanity is left
Barking dogs, cars driving pass, they're all suspect. Suicidal
homicidal, can't keep still, oh catastrophe. I have
nothing…Pity!

From home to mother's home. Displaced, dependent,
embraced the cocoon
Time begged for reflective development
With nothing to lose, I begun again
Allowing fire pits within to collaborate
Burning what worry once said
Butterflies paving the way
From mother's home to where I've always been, home

EARTH OR SEED

Clear as spring season
The blue sphere floated above her
Down and out, rags, loose
Symbols warn of descendants before her
Men women alike lost with
Raining keyboards, cubicles locked, and glass shattered

Wolves wait patient
PATIENCE! Don't leap too fast
Paused, fear reached for the heavy presence
And eyes an animal
Headed toward her own dissension
Farther from the pearl above her
Down, down the toilet
Too afraid of relief

Scribed life into her resentments, can'ts, and doubts
Dimmed lights, closets and secrets
For she so loved the earth, people in it
She drug fear so deep to call it out
Away from pearl

Like the wolves of where she used to stand, she howled
Up, in sorrow, but not at the moon
At beautiful blue pearl

DEAR DAUGHTER

You were born, I loved you. Crying out I fulfilled your needs. Cradled you in my arms late nights and early mornings. My baby girl you were always held. As you grew, your needs changed, my love did not. Believe me dear daughter, from a baby to old and gray my love for you will be always. I left behind those hugs and kisses, walks on the playground, coloring with you in your coloring books, combing your hair, and our singing duets. My life had to end there, but in your heart, there I am.

I love you. You can love you too. Remember the angel in your drawer I placed for you? The nights I'd come to visit I didn't mean to scare you. Whenever I hear my baby cry, I must show up. I see your heart beat every day, and when you think of me, I know in every way. As your heart pours in this letter from me, here I hold you. If you ever need me you know what to do. Think of the table we always sat, talked for hours while you thought you dreamt. Come as you are, you're still my baby girl. I wait on you, and hey, don't forget your shoes.

Sincerely,

Daddy

ALL MIGHTY

All and mighty
Thought you forgot about me
    Hate me
    Waste me
    Poor me

All and mighty
Thought you also forgot about me
    Love me
    Want me
    Show me

All and mighty
Thought you too forgot about me
    Support me
    Hold me
    Accept all ways, me

All and mighty
Thought I would never know
All of you, have not forgotten about me
    Thank you Thank you Thank you

OH BOY

The best day of my world
When my nights were over
Be I the son in the arms of a chunky woman
Her magnetic breasts
Seduced my lips to make me strong
Her face like my fathers
Conflicted, amused
Careful to love, love granted
And soon becoming the mourning

ABOUT THE AUTHOR

LaBrea Spivey began her journey to become an accomplished writer and poet 26 years ago when she wrote her first poem Momma Said. Inspired and amused, her expressive abilities continued to develop and ultimately became her way of investing in her own personal healing. Her poem Anna's Leap was printed in the Artifacts Nouveau Spring 2017, vol. 3.2, (A Writer's Guild publication) while she attended San Joaquin Delta College. "She mixes alchemical magic with mythology, psychology, and "word-ology", said her former creative writing professor Paula Sheil. Her poem Fragile Strength was performed with New Dance Company of Stockton, Ca., at the 24th Annual Dancing Poetry Festival, 2017, in San Francisco, Ca. Her undergraduate academic education is in Psychology. She has professional and personal experience with trauma, loss, and psychological healing.

www.ingramcontent.com/pod-product-compliance
Lightning Source LLC
Chambersburg PA
CBHW022153090426
42742CB00010B/1502
9780692073438